W9-BGE-805

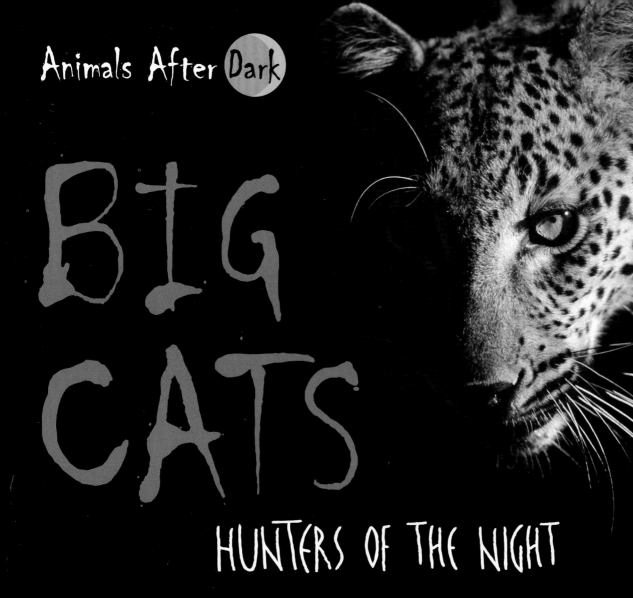

Animals After Dark

BIG CATS

HUNTERS OF THE NIGHT

Elaine Landau

WORDS TO KNOW

camouflage—An animal's coloring that helps it blend with its habitat.

carnivores—Meat eaters.

extinct—To have died out; a type of animal becomes extinct when all of its members die.

habitat—The place in which an animal lives.

mammal—An animal with a backbone that nurses its young.

prey—An animal that is hunted by another animal for food.

pride—A group of lions that live together.

prowl—To move about quietly and secretly.

savanna—A grassy plain.

stalk—To watch and follow prey from a distance.

CONTENTS

IN THE RAIN FOREST

It is nearly dark in the rain forest. A large hungry jaguar is on the prowl. Slowly it moves through the forest's thick vines and brush. It is searching for food.

Finally, the jaguar spots a deer. The large cat quietly creeps up on it and waits behind some bushes. Then it jumps! The deer has no chance of escape. The large cat holds it down with its razor-sharp claws. Seconds later, it bites into the deer.

The deer is killed with a single bite. This powerful jaguar hunter has found its meal.

A jaguar waits in the bushes, ready to strike.

A leopard lets out a mighty roar.

A LOOK AT BIG CATS

The jaguar is a big cat. "Big cat" can mean different things. However, scientists often say big cats are cats that roar. Only four cats do that—lions, tigers, leopards, and jaguars. This group of animals is called *Panthera* (PAN-thair-a).

Big cats have more in common than their roar. All big cats are very large. A male lion can be about nine feet long from head to tail. A tiger can weigh five hundred pounds or about as much as sixty house cats!

Big cats belong to a group of mammals called carnivores. Carnivores have special teeth for cutting meat. Big cats have powerful jaws and razor-sharp claws. Their four long, pointed front teeth are called canines. These help to hold their prey. Other teeth toward the back, called carnassials (kar-nas-ee-als), rip apart the prey.

high. Their long tails help them keep their balance. Most big cats are great climbers and swimmers. Only lions do not swim or climb trees.

Big cats are also smart. Their brains are large for their body size. They know the distance between them and other animals. This helps in hunting.

Yet big cats are not always on the move. They spend quite a bit of time napping. These animals usually rest during the day and become active at night.

This tiger rests during the day.

BIG CATS HAVE COATS

This snow leopard blends in well with its habitat.

A big cat's coat, or fur, blends in well with its **habitat**. This is known as **camouflage**. A tiger's stripes are hard to see in the forest's shadows. The lion's tan fur matches the tan, dried grass in African grasslands.

Leopards and jaguars rely on camouflage, too. Leopards often watch for their prey in trees. Their spotted coats blend with the leaves, making them hard to see. Some leopards and jaguars are born with black coats, which makes them very hard to see after dark. This helps in night hunting.

Big cats keep their coats very clean. They lick their fur with their rough tongues. A big cat's tongue is covered with tiny spikes. The spikes act like a comb, pulling out dirt along with any loose hairs.

NIGHT LIFE

Big cats are active mostly at night. These animals see well in the dark. They can also hear sounds that humans cannot. They can turn their ears toward a sound and tell just where it is coming from. This can be quite useful when hunting after dark.

A big cat's whiskers help at night, too. Whiskers act as "feelers." They help a cat tell if something is close by in the dark.

Lions are most active at night.

A female leopard guards her prey.

NATURAL HUNTERS

Big cats are good hunters. Some stalk their prey—they quietly follow their victim from a distance. Others wait in hiding for an animal. Then they jump on their prey. They quickly pull it to the ground.

Lions, leopards, and tigers usually bite the animal's throat. This crushes its neck so it cannot breathe. Jaguars most often bite their prey's skull to kill it.

Big cats often drag their dead prey to a private spot. Leopards and jaguars sometimes drag their victims up a tree. There they can enjoy their meal without other animals trying to steal their food.

WHERE THE BIG CATS LIVE

A male and female lion finish their daytime rest as the sun sets. The lions are in the grasslands of Kenya, a country in Africa.

Lions and leopards live in Africa and Asia. Leopards live in forests, grasslands, mountains, and deserts. Lions, on the other hand, mostly live in grassy plains called **savannas**. They also live in open woodlands.

Tigers are only found in Asia. However, these animals can live in lots of different places. There are tigers in the freezing cold areas of Siberia as well as in hot rain forests.

Jaguars are the only big cats in the Americas. They mostly live near water in rain forests and swampy grasslands.

Most big cats live and hunt alone. Only the lion lives in groups called **prides**. All cats mark the area they live in. They do this by scratching trees to leave their scent. They also urinate or leave their droppings.

Big cats often roar to warn other cats to stay away. Some nights, a whole pride of lions may roar. A lion's roar can be heard for miles.

STAYING ALIVE

For the most part, big cats have no enemies in the wild. However, at times, male lions kill the cubs of other males. This can happen when a new male takes over a pride. He then mates with the females and they have his cubs.

Tigers do not live in groups. But male tigers will also sometimes kill the cubs of other males. Then they mate with the female.

Humans are the greatest danger to big cats. Hunting these cats is against the law in many places. However, these laws are not always obeyed.

Big cats, such as this jaguar, need to be protected from harm.

MATING

All big cats mate in much the same way. When the female is ready, she gives off a special scent. This draws the male to her. The female lets the male know that she wants to mate by rolling playfully on the ground.

Within months after mating, the female gives birth to cubs.

A female lion gives off a special scent to attract a male lion.

RAISING YOUNG

A leopard cub learns
to climb.

Big cats are helpless at birth. They drink their mother's milk for their first few months. During this time, their mother also keeps them safe. Young cubs are easy prey for larger animals.

Usually two to three cubs are born. But sometimes there may be as many as five or six. As the cubs get older, they watch their mother hunt. During this time, the playful cubs practice stalking small birds and insects.

After about two years, big cats begin to hunt alone. At this point, they are ready to live on their own.

Humans are the big cats' greatest enemy. People clear forests and jungles to make way for towns and farms. Many big cats lose their habitats this way. Sometimes these animals wander into areas where people live, looking for food. They are often killed.

Big cats are also killed for their fur. People pay a lot of money for leopard coats. Tigers are sometimes killed for their body parts. This is against the law in most countries, but some people wrongly believe that a tiger's body parts can cure sicknesses.

Big cats are also killed for sport. This is usually against the law.

People sometimes put big cats like this lion in zoos.

IN THE FUTURE

As humans kill big cats, there are fewer and fewer of these animals. Some types of big cats could become extinct. However, people are trying to save them.

Countries have passed laws that make it a crime to kill or harm these animals. They also have made the punishments harsher for lawbreakers.

Some zoos are breeding big cats to increase their numbers. Some people hope to save large areas of these animals' habitats, too. Hopefully, these graceful, beautiful animals will be with us in the future.

This Siberian tiger and other tigers like it are in danger of dying out. The tiger will be trained to live in the wild before it is let go.

Tigers like to attack their prey from behind.

FUN FACTS ABOUT BIG CATS

- ⭐ The African lion spends up to twenty hours a day sleeping or resting.

- ⭐ A tiger can eat about forty pounds of meat in a meal.

- ⭐ A leopard's spots are like a person's fingerprints. No two leopards have exactly the same pattern.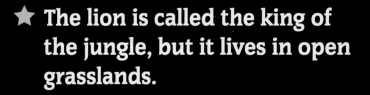

- ⭐ The lion is called the king of the jungle, but it lives in open grasslands.

- ⭐ Tigers only live in Asia. There are no tigers in Africa.

- ⭐ Tigers do not like to attack from the front. To avoid being attacked by tigers, jungle workers wear face masks on the backs of their heads. That way, a tiger always thinks the person is facing it.

TO KNOW MORE ABOUT BIG CATS

BOOKS

Cooper, Jason. *Tigers.* Vero Beach, Fla.: Rourke, 2003.

Dineen, Jacqueline. *Lions.* Mankato, Minn.: Smart Apple Media, 2004.

Gordon, Sharon. *Guess Who Roars.* New York: Benchmark Books, 2004.

Greenberg, Dan. *Leopards.* Tarrytown, N.Y.: Benchmark Books, 2003.

Squire, Ann O. *Jaguars.* Danbury, Conn.: Children's Press, 2005.

INTERNET ADDRESSES

San Diego Zoo's Animal Bytes
Fun facts about big cats.
<http://www.sandiegozoo.org/ animalbytes/>

Click on "Mammal" under "Animal categories." At the left, you can select "Jaguar," "Leopard," "Lion," or "Tiger."

Save the Tiger Fund
Visit for facts about tigers. Don't miss the kids' link; there are fun games and poetry.
<http://www.savethetigerfund. org>

Enslow Elementary, an imprint of Enslow Publishers, Inc.

Enslow Elementary® is a registered trademark of Enslow Publishers, Inc.

Library of Congress Cataloging-in-Publication Data

Landau, Elaine.
    Big cats : hunters of the night / Elaine Landau.
      p. cm. — (Animals after dark)
    Includes bibliographical references and index.
    ISBN-13: 978-0-7660-2770-1
    ISBN-10: 0-7660-2770-8
    1. Felidae—Juvenile literature. I. Title. II. Series: Landau, Elaine.
Animals after dark.
QL737.C23L355 2007
599.75'5—dc22   2006016805

Printed in the United States of America

10 9 8 7 6 5 4 3 2

To Our Readers: We have done our best to make sure all Internet Addresses in this book were active and appropriate when we went to press. However, the author and the publisher have no control over and assume no liability for the material available on those Internet sites or on other Web sites they may link to. Any comments or suggestions can be sent by e-mail to comments@enslow.com or to the address on the back cover.

Series Literacy Advisor: Dr. Allan A. De Fina, Department of Literacy Education, New Jersey City University.

Illustration Credits: Alan and Sandy Carey/Photo Researchers, Inc., pp. 4–5; © Fritz Polking/Visuals Unlimited, pp. 14–15; Gert Johannes Jacobus Very, Shutterstock.com, p. 13; Getty Images, pp. 1, 26; © iStockphoto.com/ Marco Kopp, pp. 6–7; © iStockphoto.com/Mark Nelson, pp. 2 (right), 28; © Joe McDonald/Visuals Unlimited, pp. 22–23; © 2006 Jupiter Images, p. 2 (top and bottom left), 3, 8–9, 18–19, 20–21, 25, 29, 32; Tim Fitzharris, © 2003–2005 Minden Pictures, pp. 10–11; © WorldFoto/ Alamy, pp. 16–17.

Cover Illustration: Getty Images (front and back).

Enslow Elementary
an imprint of
Enslow Publishers, Inc.
40 Industrial Road
Box 398
Berkeley Heights, NJ 07922
USA
http://www.enslow.com